Great GHOST TOWNS

of the WEST

Photography by TOM TILL ✷ *Essay by* TERESA JORDAN

GRAPHIC ARTS CENTER PUBLISHING®

Book compilation © MMI by Graphic Arts Center
  Publishing®
An imprint of Graphic Arts Center Publishing
  Company
P.O. Box 10306, Portland, Oregon 97296-0306
503/226-2402   www.gacpc.com

Library of Congress Cataloging-in-Publication Data
Till, Tom.
    Great ghost towns of the West / photographs
  by Tom Till ; text by Teresa Jordan.
      p. cm.
    Includes bibliographical references (p.) and index.
    ISBN 1-55868-521-9 (alk. paper)
      1. Ghost towns—West (U.S.) 2. Ghost towns
  —West (U.S.)—Pictorial works. 3. West
  (U.S.)—History, Local. 4. Frontier and pioneer
  life—West (U.S.) I. Jordan, Teresa. II. Title.
  F590.7.T55 2001
  978—dc21   00-068137

President: Charles M. Hopkins
Associate Publisher: Douglas A. Pfeiffer
Editorial Staff: Timothy W. Frew, Ellen Harkins Wheat,
  Tricia Brown, Kathy Matthews, Jean Andrews,
  Jean Bond-Slaughter
Production Staff: Richard L. Owsiany, Heather
  Doornink
Design: Elizabeth Watson
Map: Gray Mouse Graphics
Digital pre-press and printing: Haagen Printing
Binding: Lincoln & Allen

Printed in the United States of America

Photographs: Page 1: *Adobe ruins at Swansea, Arizona.*
3: *Guard's room in the assay office in Vulture, Arizona.*
4: *Paintbrush in Holy Cross City, Colorado.*
6: *Tinton, South Dakota.*
7: *Collapsed roof with morning frost in Tinton, South Dakota.*
8: *Thistle, Utah.*
10: *Ashcroft, Colorado.*
125: *Foamflower in Gem, Idaho, Bodie, California.*
127: *Sunflowers in Chloride, New Mexico.*
128: *Turret, Colorado.*

To my ancestors who founded the ghost town of Prichard, Idaho
—T. T.

For Hal
—T. J.

✳

ACKNOWLEDGMENTS

Many thanks to my family: Marcy, Mikenna, and Bryce. I also owe a debt of gratitude to Bodie State Park and the California State Park System; the town of Vulture, Arizona; the residents of Elkhorn, Montana; the owners of Cerro Gordo, California; the caretakers of Tinton, South Dakota, and Bay Horse, Idaho, and Kennicott Lodge in Kennicott, Alaska; and as always the National Park Service, the Bureau of Land Management, and the National Forest Service.

—T. T.

My thanks go first to photographer Tom Till and publisher Doug Pfeiffer for inviting me into this project, and to editor Ellen Wheat and the rest of the Graphic Arts Center Publishing® staff for their generous and inspired support. My task was made even more enjoyable by the many friends who fed and housed me during various stages of this project, including Bob and Lynn Budd in Wyoming; John and Donna Grey in Montana; Toni Dewey and Vic Danilov in Colorado; Lynda Gilman in Washington; and Andrea Carlisle, Martha Banyas and Michael Hoeye, and Christine Bourdette and Ricardo Lovett in Oregon. My deepest gratitude is to the thousands of private landowners, large and small philanthropists, volunteers, and employees of local, state, and federal agencies who labor with love to keep these ghost towns from blowing away in the wind.

—T. J.

✳

C O N T E N T S

GREAT GHOST TOWNS of the WEST

ALASKA
1. Bonanza
2. Kennicott

ARIZONA
3. Swansea
4. Jerome
5. Vulture
6. Wickenburg
7. Cloverdale
8. Ruby
9. Tombstone
10. Bisbee

BRITISH COLUMBIA
11. Retallack
12. Sandon

CALIFORNIA
13. Timbuctoo
14. Alta
15. Marysville
16. Columbia

17. Jamestown
18. Bodie
19. Copperopolis
20. Death Valley
21. Cerro Gordo
22. Randsburg
23. Calico

COLORADO
24. Crystal
25. Leadville
26. Georgetown
27. Ashcroft
28. Holy Cross City
29. Turret
30. Tomboy
31. Placerville
32. Cripple Creek
33. Altman
34. Bent's Old Fort National Historic Site
35. St. Elmo
36. Telluride

37. Animas Forks
38. Alta
39. Carson
40. Ironton

IDAHO
41. Coeur d'Alene
42. Gem
43. Bay Horse
44. Placerville
45. Silver City
46. Chesterfield

MONTANA
47. Garnet
48. Elkhorn
49. Buffalo
50. Lewistown
51. Mildred
52. Harlowtown
53. Bozeman
54. Nevada City
55. Virginia City
56. Bannack

NEVADA
57. Virginia City
58. Marietta
59. Belmont
60. Hamilton
61. Rhyolite

NEW MEXICO
62. Elizabethtown
63. Las Trampas
64. Cerillos
65. Madrid
66. Golden
67. White Oaks
68. Chloride
69. Mogollon
70. Pinos Altos
71. Shakespeare
72. Steins

OREGON
73. Shaniko
74. Kent
75. Whitney

76. Granite

SOUTH DAKOTA
77. Tinton
78. Deadwood
79. Rochford
80. Scenic
81. Okaton

TEXAS
82. Salt Flat
83. Terlingua
84. Langtry

UTAH
85. Iosepa
86. Promontory Point
87. Park City
88. Ophir
89. Scofield
90. Eureka
91. Spring City
92. Thistle

93. Cove Fort
94. Canyonlands National Park
95. San Raphael Swell
96. Elgin
97. Cisco
98. Castletown
99. Bicknell
100. Frisco
101. Harrisburg
102. Grafton
103. Paria River

WASHINGTON
104. Molson
105. Bodie

WYOMING
106. Antelope Flats
107. South Pass City
108. Piedmont
109. Laramie

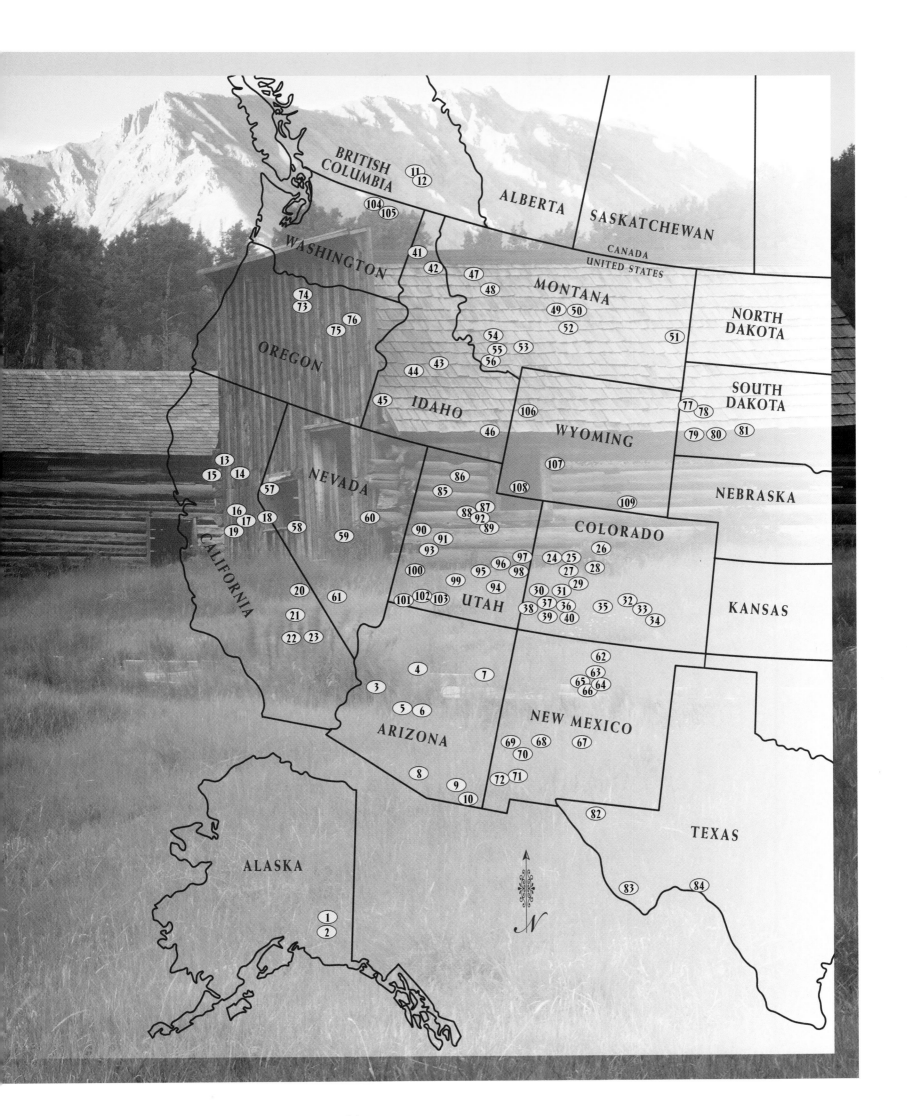

PROLOGUE

★

Left: *Over forty original buildings still stand in St. Elmo, Colorado.*
Above: *Lace curtains in St. Elmo, Colorado.*

PROLOGUE
A Gathering of Ghosts

✴

*I think no object is without the bricks of human history
weighing it down, planting it on the earth as our neighbor.
There is no weathered window without the ghost of a face behind it,
no empty stanchion in a barn without a spectral cow munching hay
and swishing her tail while a boy sits on a three-legged stool
squeezing into a pail. . . .*

—BILL HOLM, *A LANDSCAPE OF GHOSTS*

✴

EVERY SO OFTEN

I'D BE STARTLED BY A RABBIT

THAT WOULD HOP INTO THE

BANK. . . . "HOP" IS NOT

THE PROPER VERB. . . .

THEY DIDN'T HOP,

THEY "SPROINGED."

The year was 1983. I had just moved to Montana and was poking along the back roads to see what I could find. I had turned off the highway between Lewistown and Harlowton, in almost the exact center of the state. I drove toward Buffalo—a clutter of buildings, many in near collapse—and stopped before a small brick bank.

The open door seemed like a personal invitation, and I prowled around inside. Every so often I'd be startled by a rabbit that would hop into the bank and, on

✴

*Left: A door left open in the Meade home, Bannack, Montana.
Montana's first territorial capital is now maintained as the Bannack State Park.
Above: Despite a raging fire in 1912, many original buildings still
survive in the abandoned mining town of Garnet, Montana.*

✴

Above: Log cabin, Bannack, Montana.
The first gold there was panned
from nearby Grasshopper Creek in 1862.
Right: Perhaps Henry Plummer,
Bannack's notorious sheriff whose gang
killed as many as a hundred people, had
his whiskers trimmed in this chair.
Overleaf: Today, St. Elmo, Colorado, has
only one resident but is somewhat protected
from vandalism by its remoteness
in the Collegiate Range.

finding me there, just as quickly hop out. "Hop" is not the proper verb. I'd never seen rabbits like this in the West. They were multicolored and, at least in memory, as large as adolescent kangaroos. They didn't hop, they "sproinged." I heard a car approach, and stepped outside.

The car was big and old, turquoise with lots of chrome and confident fins. It stopped, the doors opened, and then very slowly an elderly couple began to extricate themselves. I went over and introduced myself. "I saw Buffalo on the map," I told them. "I just wanted to see what was here."

"Not much, anymore," the man told me with the hint of an accent. "It's yoost a ghost town." His wife chuckled and added, "We're the only ghosts left in town."

They introduced themselves as the Flugges (rhymes with "boogies") and invited me home for lemonade. I learned that Mr. Flugge had come to America on a leaky

★

Although Ironton, Colorado, is quiet now, it was once home to a thousand people.

boat from Germany. A railroad job brought him to Montana where he met his wife, a rancher's daughter. They told me that I could find ghost towns like Buffalo all along the railroad. The early steam engines needed water every few miles, and communities grew up to serve them. As engines improved, many of the towns blew away, especially those like Buffalo that had never incorporated or developed a water system.

The Flugges had watched their neighbors move away one by one, but they liked Buffalo and they liked their home even if it didn't have indoor plumbing. As the town emptied, Mr. Flugge bought up town lots. Then another local, who I'll call Mr. White, thought Mr. Flugge was onto something, and bought City Hall and the schoolhouse. He started raising pigs in the schoolhouse and domestic rabbits in City Hall, or maybe it was the other way around. At any rate, he overextended

himself. He sold his pigs but turned the rabbits loose, which explained the bounding acquaintances I'd made earlier in the day.

I had several more conversations with the Flugges over the course of the next few weeks, which remain among my richest memories of that peripatetic summer. They taught me a valuable lesson: every ghost town has a story, and some even have living—and most hospitable—ghosts.

★ ★ ★

<img src /> ★

In many mining towns, social organizations built some of the first substantial buildings, such as the Masonic Hall in Bannack, Montana.

What is it about ghost towns that so intrigues us? What draws us to abandonment and ruin, a sense of things left behind? Why are we so fascinated with ghosts?

Among the definitions for "ghost" are "a haunting memory" and "a shadowy semblance of its former self." A ghost town is both of these, and something more. When we poke around an abandoned community, we catch the scent of what it means to be human. Somehow, every dream and risk we ever attempted as well as those we didn't, every success and every failure, wafts around us. We remember the temporary nature of our time on earth, and this brings a curious satisfaction: the ones who once lived here are gone, but here *we* are, and that's something.

This book is not a guidebook; there are plenty of good ones around already.

Elkhorn, Montana, south of
Helena, is now protected by the
U.S. Forest Service and watched
over by people who live nearby.

✳

Schoolhouse in Vulture, Arizona. Mines and mining towns often took their names from the local flora and fauna, and their choices often revealed a lot about the inhabitants or the surrounding environment.

Rather, photographer Tom Till and I wanted to capture some of the mysterious essence that intrigues us about ghost towns. Tom's evocative photographs capture the *towns* in both their remnants and their auras; with luck, my words capture the *ghosts* in the stories of the people who passed through.

✶ ✶ ✶

For people to live in a place, they must make a living. This simple tautology underlies ghost towns. Towns spring up around resources like gold or good agricultural ground, or because they can provide a service, as Buffalo did to the railroad in its early years. If that resource plays out or the service is no longer needed and no new purpose replaces it, the town dies.

More ghost towns sprang up around mining than any other purpose, and they

are among the most colorful, both in story and in built environment. The lure of easy riches attracted passionate and colorful people. When they had money, they built ornate buildings. When they went broke, they left with flair. For those reasons, we will look in most detail at the mining ghosts. But the farm towns and logging towns and transportation towns bear their own wealth of stories, and we'll introduce you to some of these, too.

The Flugges have passed on, but their grandson Daniel is raising his six kids in the town, which makes Buffalo a good deal livelier today than when I first visited. Other ghost towns have made more remarkable comebacks. Park City, Utah, once listed as a ghost town, now thrives as a ski resort. And that may hint at yet another lure of abandoned communities. Who among us can walk along these spectral streets without longing to see them flourish once again?

★

Calico, California, once among the richest silver camps in the state, took its name from the colorful mountains nearby. Walter Knott, founder of Knott's Berry Farm, restored the town and gave it to San Bernadino County in 1966, which now runs it as a regional park.

-25-

GETTING THERE IS HALF THE FUN

*

Left: *Part of the old mill at Skidoo, California, high above Death Valley.*
Above: *Tattered curtains in Bodie, California.*

GETTING THERE IS HALF THE FUN

California and the
First Great Gold Rush

*My eye was caught by something shining
in the bottom of the ditch. . . . I reached my hand down and
picked it up; it made my heart thump, for I was certain it was gold.
The piece was about half the size and shape of a pea.
Then I saw another. . . .*

—JAMES MARSHALL, ABOUT HIS DISCOVERY ON JANUARY 24, 1848,
THAT STARTED THE CALIFORNIA GOLD RUSH

JAMES MARSHALL PULLED A NUGGET OF ALMOST PURE GOLD OUT OF CALIFORNIA'S AMERICAN RIVER. . . . HE SHOWED HIS DISCOVERY TO HIS EMPLOYER, JOHN SUTTER . . . AND A HOARD OF EAGER MINERS OVERRAN SUTTER'S MILL.

After James Marshall pulled a nugget of almost pure gold out of California's American River, he showed his discovery to his employer, John Sutter, a Swiss-born Mexican citizen recently arrived in California with dreams of empire, who had already acquired an expansive ranch, built his own fort, and hired an army

Left: *High in the Inyo Mountains of the Owens Valley, the silver town
of Cerro Gordo (Spanish for "fat hill") boomed in the 1870s.*
Above: *Old bedsprings rust on the overland route through Terlingua, Texas.*

"ON DOORS AND COUNTERS

THE POSTED NOTICE 'G.T.C.'

MEANT ONLY ONE THING:

'GONE TO CALIFORNIA.'"

of Indians. Sutter tried to keep the discovery quiet but rumors spread. His workers fled to prospect on their own, and a hoard of eager miners overran Sutter's Mill.

Foremost among them was Sam Brannan, recently arrived in California with a shipload of Mormons who had come prospecting not for gold but for a place of refuge. Brannan was a natural businessman. When he heard of the strike, he rushed to Sutter's Mill and opened a store. Then he started drumming up customers: he filled a quinine bottle with gold dust and headed to San Francisco, where he walked the streets crying "Gold! Gold! Gold from the American River."

That was in mid-May 1848; within a month, three-fourths of the city's male population had fled for the goldfields. Empty ships sagged at anchor, doors swung open on abandoned stores and government offices, schools closed for want of teachers, the Presidio lost its soldiers en masse as they fled with the officers' horses. When the word spread north, two-thirds of Oregon's able-bodied men answered the call; the legislature suspended for lack of a quorum, and the territorial newspapers shut down with no one to run the presses.

But during that first year, the California gold rush was something of a West Coast phenomenon and the living was easy. One miner, nagged about a debt, said "wait ten minutes and time me," headed into the night with his pickaxe, and returned before his time expired with gold for his creditor. Another, in the heat of a high-stakes poker hand, asked a buddy to watch his pile "until I go out and dig enough to call him." Gold was so plentiful that "thousands of dollars were left in tents unguarded." Or so said the lore of the times.

All that changed within a year. After President James Polk announced the discovery in his annual message to Congress, gold fever gripped the nation. "In store windows and newspaper ads," wrote the historian Remi Nadeau, "every

conceivable commodity was labeled with the magic word 'California.' There were 'California hats,' 'California pistols,' even 'California pork and beans.' On doors and counters the posted notice 'G.T.C.' meant only one thing: 'Gone to California.'"

✱   ✱   ✱

Getting there, as the saying goes, is half the fun. With the transcontinental railroad still twenty years in the future, crossing the continent was torturous. The emigrant had three primary routes to choose from: around Cape Horn, eighteen thousand miles and four to six months of storms and sea sickness; across the Isthmus of Panama, an adventure of a few weeks if everything went well, or several months when it didn't; or across the continent by overland trail, the route most often preferred by landlubbers.

The brutal seas around the Cape had long been treacherous. Once gold fever struck, anything that would float set out for California, and the Cape became a graveyard for ships. Even on more seaworthy vessels, the passengers suffered a sort of purgatory: unbearably cramped quarters, rampant disease, and endless rough seas.

But such concerns were the least of it for Captain and Mrs. Bates, sailing from Baltimore in 1850. After a storm kept his wife in their cabin for three days, the captain learned that his cargo of coal was smoldering. While the crew battened down the hatches and caulked the seams, the captain steamed for the nearest shore—the Falkland Islands, eight hundred miles away—and Mrs. Bates lashed herself to a chair topside and braved the storm, the only alternative to death by suffocation. On the Falklands, they caught another coal freighter headed to Valparaiso. A few days later they found themselves "eighty miles from

✱

Nearly 150 buildings remain in Bodie, California, making it one of the most fascinating ghost towns around. The California State Park Service now maintains it in a state of "arrested decay."

★

Above: A miner's cabin in Alta, Colorado. The only way to reach this mountain ghost town in the winter is on skis or by snowmobile.
Page 34: Although only a few buildings remain in Alta, Colorado, the town pioneered the industrial use of alternating current in 1891, installed with the help of Nikola Tesla and George Westinghouse.

land, and, horror of horrors, the ship on fire!" When it burst into flames, the Bateses and other passengers escaped in a lifeboat and were picked up by another steamer. The good news was that it was headed for San Francisco. The bad news? It was carrying coal. In a few days, an all-too-familiar scent filled the air: Another three weeks of high drama found them disembarked in Peru, just before, once again, their ship exploded in flames. Ever game, the captain and his wife caught a fourth ship, landed in California, and struck it rich in the hotel business.

On paper at least, the easier route was across Panama. You had only to set sail from the East, arrive a few weeks later, in Chagres on the east coast of Panama, spend the night in the luxurious Astor House or Crescent City Hotel (in reality, bamboo huts), dine on baked monkey, and leave the next day for a week-long trek by foot, mule, and *bungo* (a wood canoe piloted by a Native) to Panama City, where another steamer carried you the rest of the way to San Francisco. But malaria lurked in the jungle, cholera on both coasts. Occasionally Natives or disgruntled emigrants robbed and murdered people on the trail.

The real snag came in Panama City. So many clamored to sail to San Francisco, and so many ships that had once carried passengers up and down the coast stood abandoned by their gold-hungry crews in San Francisco harbor (some six hundred of them by the end of 1849), that argonauts often had to wait months before they could leave Panama, and the delay cost them. Howard C. Gardiner left New York in March of 1849 with $475 and arrived in San Francisco more than four months later with empty pockets.

William Swain's Overland Journey

William Swain left his wife, baby daughter, and brother in Youngstown, New York, in April 1849, hoping to return with enough California gold to change his family's prospects forever. He joined the Wolverine Rangers, a Michigan party that thought they had plenty of time to reach the goldfields before winter. But cholera, short feed for their teams, breakdowns, and bad weather slowed them down.

They reached what is now western Nevada in late September, spooked by reports of the desert when they turned south. They also heard of a new trail, Lassen's Cut-off, which promised an easier route. Never mind that no first-hand account of the route existed; the Rangers, as well as virtually all the emigrants from mid-August on, turned away from known horrors to embrace a geography based mostly on hope.

They stumbled into a nightmare. First they had to cross the Black Rock Desert: more than forty miles of thirst and desolation littered by an ever-widening trail of carcasses. When they headed into the mountains, dead oxen lined the trail that climbed to over ten thousand feet, but Swain's party rejoiced to reach the summit in good shape.

Their joy was short lived. Instead of looking down into the Sacramento Valley, they saw before them a "labyrinth of mountains." They were not in the Sierras at all but in what we now know as the Warner Range, more than two hundred miles from their destination. It was mid-October and snowing.

Nearly eight thousand emigrants were caught in the mountains by then. Army relief parties met them and begged them to abandon everything and run for their lives. But it took three more weeks before Swain and his party, caught in a blizzard, finally jettisoned their wagons and stumbled through "pathetic camps of men stricken with scurvy, too weak to move; carcasses of oxen bloody from butchering by emigrants hungry for meat."

Swain arrived in the Sacramento Valley and encamped "without fire and with every thread of clothes wet, sheltered from the rain by only my blanket. . . ." He would have to wait out the winter before seeking gold. As another in his party wrote home, "You will shed tears when you come to know how much I have suffered and the hardships I have encountered. If it had not been for you and the children to think of, I should certainly have given up and died."

✶

Background: *Marietta, Nevada, with Boundary Peak,*
the state's highest mountain, in the distance.

✳

Overleaf: *The fifteen stamps that once crushed gold ore still remain at this mill in Skidoo, California. Water to operate the mill traveled by pipeline from a spring twenty-three miles away.*
Above: *Some of the original "plumbing" in Bodie, California, is on the verge of collapse.*

✳ ✳ ✳

The hardest trek was overland by emigrant train, though it was also the most popular, especially with gold seekers who had no experience with the sea. These landlubbers leaned to the familiar, and they pored over handbooks written by earlier pioneers on the Oregon and California Trails. They thought they knew what lay in store for them. In 1850, twenty-five thousand people crossed the continent to search for California gold; twice that number in 1851. The majority of them were men, but some women and families went as well. If they survived cholera, breakdowns, storms, and dissension as far as Salt Lake City, they faced even greater challenges on the desert.

Juliette Brier was thirty-five years old when she traveled with her husband, three young sons, and thirty-four other men from Illinois. Four of the party died crossing Death Valley; the Brier family survived, but Juliette Brier recorded how two days without water had tortured her oldest son:

> The child would murmur occasionally, "Oh, father, where's the water." His pitiful, delirious wails were worse to hear than the killing thirst. . . . I staggered and struggled wearily behind with the other two boys and the oxen. The little fellows bore up bravely and hardly complained, though they could barely talk, so dry and swollen were their lips and tongue. . . . Every step I expected to sink down and die.

By the time the Briers arrived in California, Juliette's husband had lost one hundred pounds. But for them, like the others who survived the journey, the adventure had just begun.

Native Ghosts

When we think of deserted mining communities, we usually picture the ghosts as Euro-American miners and their various contemporaries of many nationalities and races. But these are really "second generation" ghosts, for they tread on landscapes once peopled by others: the Native Americans that mining rushes not only displaced but destroyed.

Long before gold was found by non-Natives in California, the region's indigenous people had suffered at the hands of newcomers. During the years of Mexican rule and missionary zeal, 1822–46, somewhere between twenty-five and fifty thousand died. " 'They live well free,' a puzzled friar said, 'but as soon as we reduce them to a Christian and community life . . . they fatten, sicken, and die.' " But the onslaught of '49ers pushed Indians from their homelands, destroyed their food sources, brought new and devastating diseases, and often murdered the Indians outright.

Shocked by stories of mistreatment, federal commissioners negotiated treaties with eighteen tribes that would have ceded 8.5 million acres for sanctuary, but the California delegation assured that the treaties failed in the U.S. Senate. Twenty years after gold was discovered in California, the region's indigenous population had declined from 150,000 to 30,000, the single worst devastation of Indian people in our nation's history. Similarly, in Colorado, in Nevada, in the Southwest, in the Black Hills—the cry of "Gold!" foretold disaster for Natives.

Background: *Weathered wood siding in Cerro Gordo, California.*

HOME IS WHERE YOU HANG YOUR HAT

Left: *The W. Duncan home in Animas Forks, Colorado.*
Above: *Door of the J. S. Cain home in Bodie, California.*

HOME IS WHERE YOU HANG YOUR HAT

Creating Shelter and Community

Really, everybody ought to go to the mines, just to see how little it takes to make people comfortable in the world.

— DAME SHIRLEY (LOUISA CLAPP), *CALIFORNIA CHRONICLER*, 1850

DR. J. B. STILLMAN,

WHO WORKED IN THE

CALIFORNIA GOLDFIELDS,

ESTIMATED THAT AS MANY AS

20 PERCENT OF THE MINERS

DIED WITHIN SIX MONTHS

OF ARRIVING.

Gold! It's hard to imagine anything in our contemporary lives grabbing us like gold fever seized our forebears in the nineteenth and early twentieth centuries. Miners often arrived at a new strike so eager that, as one witness recorded, they "went to work . . . without tents, many without blankets to shield them from the cold night air. . . . Hundreds have been stricken down by disease." Dr. J. B. Stillman, who worked in the California goldfields, estimated that as many as 20 percent of the miners died within six months of arriving.

Quickly, however, shelter became imperative, and more permanent communities sprang up with amazing speed. Seasoned by the California experience, merchants,

Left: *The Lottie Johl house, Bodie, California.*
Above: *Hotel in Cerro Gordo, California, built in 1871.*

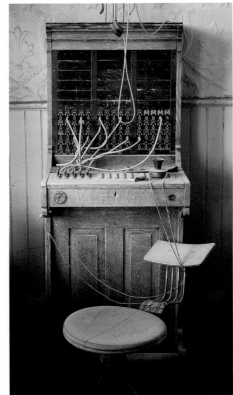

freighters, and hoteliers in later strikes knew just what miners needed, and when news of a promising camp leaked out, relatively sophisticated services sprang up overnight. "Enterprising men hurried to the spot with barrels of whiskey and billiard tables," wrote journalist J. Ross Browne, observing the gestation of Gila City after gold was found in 1858 in what is now Arizona. "Jews came with ready-made clothing and fancy wares; traders crowded in with wagonloads of pork and beans; and gamblers came with cards and monte tables. There was everything in Gila City within a few months but a church and a jail, which were accounted barbarisms by the mass of the population."

With rare exception, the populations of the new camps were predominantly

✳

Left: *The Jersey Lily Saloon in Langtry, Texas. Some believe that the town was named after a civil engineer, but Judge Roy Bean claimed he named the town after Lillie Langtry, the English actress known as the Jersey Lily.*
Above (clockwise): *Artifacts in Bodie, California, include bottles, W. & H. telephone, mail sorter, and store shelves.*

★

Mannequin in the Boone Store and Warehouse, Bodie, California. Harvey Boone, a direct descendant of Daniel Boone, started his business in 1879.

male and usually young. "I cannot recall ever seeing a man with white hair," recalled one veteran. Surely he exaggerated, but youth and a lack of social constraints combined to create a freewheeling atmosphere. Kevin Starr, the state historian of California, likens his region's early days to a great fraternity party, a term that might be apt for Animas Forks in Colorado's San Juan Mountains. When a twenty-three-day storm in 1884 left twenty-five feet of snow on the ground, "the miners holed up

✦

Above: *Pool table and roulette wheel,
Wheaton and Hollis Hotel, Bodie, California.
Left: Roulette wheel in the Sam Leon Bar,
Bodie, California. The devil-may-care
rowdiness of miners has been celebrated
since the earliest days of the gold rush, which
may be why, when word leaked out that
one little girl en route to Bodie with her family
had written in her diary, "Goodbye, God,
I'm going to Bodie," the phrase became
famous throughout the West.*

the winter in the saloon and kept the economy going by beating each other at poker," though this particular party included three women and twenty dogs.

Many early mining towns took a sort of heathen glee in their wild reputations. Frontier memoirist Anne Ellis noted that "in speaking of population, you didn't count people, . . . you counted saloons and dance-halls," and a coroner's jury in California stated that the cause of death for a man poisoned by alcohol was "death

★

*W. Duncan home, Animas Forks,
Colorado. At 11,200 feet, winters
can be hard; in 1884, 25 feet of snow
fell here in 23 days.*

by hanging—round a rum-shop." However exciting these early, wild days, the miners themselves seemed to hanker after something a bit more civilized, if the speed with which successful mining camps matured is any indication.

Such was the case for Virginia City, Nevada Territory, which the omnipresent J. Ross Browne described in the spring of 1860 as nothing more than "frame shanties, pitched together as if by accident; tents of canvas, of blankets, of brush, of potato-sacks and old shirts, with empty whiskey barrels for chimneys." Three years later, he returned to find three- and four-story brick buildings in place. Once so wild that a

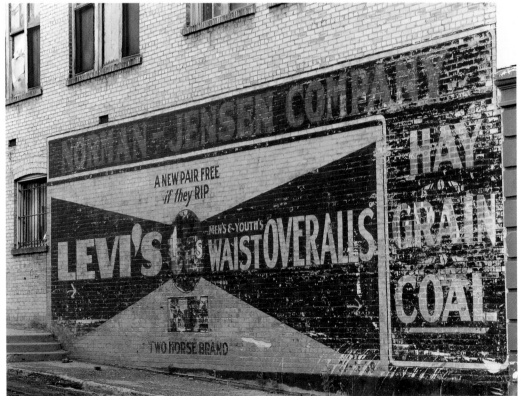

Above: *Opera house in Pinos Altos,*
New Mexico. With money to spend and
starved for entertainment, miners enjoyed
the arts wherever they could find them.
Left: *Advertisement in Eureka, Utah.*
The rigors of mining spawned many
inventions that are with us today including
Levi's jeans, a joint venture between
San Francisco retailer Levi Strauss and
Reno, Nevada, tailor Jacob Davis.

group of vigilantes formed and ended a crime wave by hanging some twenty-four
blackguards, by 1864 the *Montana Post* reported that "100 buildings are being
erected each week in Virginia City and its environs." By the end of the decade the
town sported churches of several denominations and a thriving business district
with at least eleven Jewish merchants. It had opened Montana's first public school,
a public skating rink, and clubs ranging from a Masonic Lodge to the Montana
Historical Society to the African American Pioneer Social Club.

When miners turned into millionaires, they were quick to adopt the styles of

Color

A visit to an unrestored ghost town will probably leave you with the impression that these were drab places to spend the winter. Not necessarily so. Many mining camp observers commented on the ubiquitous red cotton used for everything from clothing to tablecloths to upholstery to wall covering. Red was not confined to interiors. *Leslie's Weekly* deemed Altman, Colorado, "garish" in the late nineteenth century because of the red building paper used as siding. Nor was red the only spate of color. The Empire Hotel in Rich Bar, California, was a claptrap affair with floors "so very uneven that you are always ascending a hill or descending into a valley," but it nonetheless enjoyed rich attention to color. As writer Dame Shirley described it, "The entire building is lined with purple calico, alternating with a delicate blue, and the effect is really quite pretty."

Background: *Inside a decaying cabin with peeling wallpaper in Tomboy, Colorado.*

✳

Above: *Lottie Johl house, Bodie, California. Mrs. Johl worked in the red light district before she married her husband, a butcher. She became a respected painter.*
Left: *Mess hall, Vulture, Arizona. Commissaries sprang up quickly to serve the large number of single miners.*
Overleaf: *Time and vandals have taken their toll in Tinton, South Dakota, which is now posted against trespassing.*

Paris and New York in their food, clothes, furnishings, and entertainment. Stonemason H. A. W. Tabor, for instance, built opera houses in Leadville and Denver after he struck it rich. Hotel de Paris in Georgetown, Colorado, was filled with ornate walnut furniture, bottled its own wine, and served such delicacies as oysters on the half shell, quail, truffles, and trout freshly snagged from its outdoor fountain.

But great wealth was not prerequisite to a hankering for culture. Sometimes this grew out of a simple yearning for entertainment. Oscar Wilde's lectures in Leadville, Colorado, were hugely attended, though not, according to one Colorado scribe, because of a widespread interest in literature. Rather, Wilde had captivated Leadville by drinking a group of miners under the table. On the other hand, just a year after South Pass City was founded in 1867 in Wyoming Territory, it built an

Assay office, Cerro Gordo, California.
Some $13 million worth of silver and lead
was shipped from here between 1868 and
1875, much of it in steamboats.

opera house that soon attracted a performance of *Lucretia Borgia* by the Carter Troupe.

The West had as many as one hundred thousand mining districts by 1900. Some of them never evolved beyond the tent-and-shanty stage and can be located today only by a keen eye for archaeology; others became sophisticated small cities. Isolation has historically worked against mining towns, but now it is often their

A Husband Wanted

By a lady who can wash, cook, scour, sew, milk, spin, weave, hoe, (can't plow), cut wood, make fires, feed the pigs, raise chickens, rock the cradle (gold-rocker, I thank you Sir!), saw a plank, drive nails, etc. These are a few of the solid branches; now for the ornamental. . . . Could read, and you can see she can write. Can—no, could—paint roses, butterflies, ships, etc. Could once dance. . . . Oh, I hear you ask, could she scold? No, she can't you, you _____ good-for-nothing _____!

Now for her terms. Her age is none of your business. She is neither handsome nor a fright, yet an old man need not apply, nor any who have not a little more education than she has, and a great deal more gold, for there must be $20,000 settled on her before she will bind herself to perform all the above. Address to DOROTHY SCRAGGS, with real name. P.O. Marysville."

— AD IN A MARYSVILLE, CALIFORNIA, NEWSPAPER, 1849

Background: *Kitchen in Bodie, California.*

★

Above and right: *Assay office, Vulture,*
Arizona. This room saw a lot of excitement:
the Vulture Mine was Arizona's richest,
producing over $200 million in gold.

salvation, as people increasingly interested in recreation escape from city life.
Historic preservation has breathed life into many "ghosts" that only a few years ago
seemed ready to return to the soil out of which they were raised.

One Woman's Funeral

I have just returned from the funeral of poor Mrs. B., who died of peritonitis . . . after an illness of four days only. . . .

On a board, supported by two butter-tubs, was extended the body of the dead woman, covered with a sheet; by its side stood the coffin of unstained pine, lined with white cambric. . . . About twenty men, with the three women of the place, had assembled at the funeral. An extempore prayer was made, filled with all the peculiarities usual to that style of petition. . . .

I almost forgot to tell you, how painfully the feelings of the assembly were shocked by the sound of the nails—there being no screws at any of the shops—driven with a hammer into the coffin, while closing it. It seemed as if it must disturb the pale sleeper within."

— DAME SHIRLEY (LOUISE CLAPPE),
THE SHIRLEY LETTERS FROM THE CALIFORNIA MINES, 1851–52

✳

Background: *Violin in morgue, Bodie, California.*

HI, HO! HI, HO! IT'S OFF TO WORK WE GO

Left: *Bonanza Mine, Wrangell–St. Elias National Park and Preserve, Alaska.*
Above: *The view from Alta, Colorado.*

HI, HO! HI, HO! IT'S OFF TO WORK WE GO

Dreams and Drudgery on the Western Frontier

*I will tell you this mining among the mountains is a dog's life.
A man has to make a jackass of himself packing loads over mountains
that God never designed man to climb, a barbarian by foregoing
all the comforts of civilized life, and a heathen by depriving himself
of all communication with men away from his immediate circle.*

—WILLIAM SWAIN, ON THE SOUTH FORK OF THE FEATHER RIVER,
CALIFORNIA, 1850

ANYONE COULD AFFORD

THE EQUIPMENT—A PAN COST

ONLY A DOLLAR OR TWO,

A PICK AND SHOVEL MAYBE

SIX DOLLARS APIECE.

The easiest mining—that which lured Everyman and a good many women from all corners of the earth to California, to Colorado, to the Black Hills, to the Klondike—is placer mining (pronounced "plasser"), or panning for gold. Anyone could afford the equipment—a pan cost only a dollar or two, a pick and shovel

Left: *Mill in Crystal City, Colorado.*
Above: *Jerome, Arizona. According to legend, the Sinagua Indians
first discovered copper here over a thousand years ago.*

★

Above: *Retallack, British Columbia,
is one of several old mining towns in the
Valley of the Ghosts in the beautiful
Kokanee Range of the Selkirk Mountains.
Right: Gold and silver lured miners
to Carson, Colorado; at some twelve
thousand feet high up in the San Juan
Mountains, it is one of the most
inaccessible places in Colorado.*

maybe six dollars apiece. A hard worker could swirl about fifty pans a day; if he averaged gold worth ten cents a try he broke even, gold-rush prices not withstanding. When a good claim combined with good luck, a single pan might yield fifty dollars or more. When panning proved too tedious, miners banded together in groups and operated rockers or "long toms," sluice boxes with riffles on the bottom that caught the gold particles as the diggers shoveled in load after load of sand and gravel.

But placer gold was surface gold and didn't last long. The next option was to dig down in the riverbed to bedrock where gold might have lodged. Sometimes bedrock was close to the surface; more often it lay under tens of feet—and hundreds of tons—of rubble. To claim it, the river had to be diverted, a shaft sunk, and drifts or tunnels dug radiating out from the shaft along the bedrock. This took both money and manpower, and "coyote-diggings" could take months to pay out— if they paid out at all.

Other methods were even more intensive. Hydraulic mining used jets of water to wash whole hillsides away, and by 1857, more than four thousand miles of flumes and ditches drained the California mountains at a cost of nearly twelve million dollars. Quartz mining blasted tunnels into the sides of mountains and sunk shafts deep into their bowels. Stamp mills, to pulverize the quartz and free the gold, cost in excess of fifty to a hundred thousand dollars; nine-tenths of these operations failed, and the abandoned machinery can be found at many a ghost town today.

★

Gigantic mill in Kennicott ghost town in the Wrangell–St. Elias National Park and Preserve, Alaska. Kennicott is second only to Bodie, California, as a great ghost town, and its location, in our biggest national park, is extraordinary.

The stamp mills, like the miles of flumes, indicated the change in mining from the pursuit of lone wolves and small partnerships to one of industrialists and paid laborers. Many independent '49ers scorned working for wages and rushed off to new finds in British Columbia, Nevada, and Colorado. In mining frontier after mining frontier, when industrial mining replaced placers, prospectors moved on to the next excitement while their less adventurous compatriots drew paychecks and spent them at the company store.

Place Names

When a mining district organized, one of its first tasks was to name itself, and names came from any number of sources. Most obvious are those from natural resources: Gold Camp, Silver City, Leadville, and the melodious Copperopolis. Hopes and dreams often came into play: Eureka, Bonanza, El Dorado, Miner's Delight or, more whimsically, Small Hopes, What Cheer, and Oh Be Joyful. The character and even politics of the founders often found its way onto the map: Delirium Tremens, Wide Awake, Unionville, Dixie Flats. Many place names reflected their founders' ethnic origins or hometowns: German Bar, Dublin Gulch, Chinese Camp, Baltimore, Boston, and Bunker Hill. Stories underlie any number of names. Cripple Creek, Colorado, earned its title when a miner accidentally shot another man in the foot. To compound the first injury, the gunshot and the injured man's swearing so frightened a calf that it leapt across the creek, breaking its leg. Sometimes the story isn't what you might imagine. Timbuctoo, California, was not named ironically for its isolation, but rather belongs in the "longing for home" category. A refugee Southern slave found the first gold there and named the place after Timbuktu, his hometown in Africa.

Background: *This one-time tourist attraction at Two Guns, Arizona, on Route 66, once displayed captive mountain lions and other exotic creatures.*

✳

Bonanza Mine, Wrangell–St. Elias
National Park and Preserve, Alaska.
Only a die-hard hiker can reach these
remote remains near Kennicott.

✳

As mining became more complicated, it also became more dangerous. The placer miner, standing as he did from dawn to dusk in high mountain streams, was more likely to die of illness than injury. Mining became more deadly when it moved underground. On Nevada's Comstock Lode, where the large, unstable ore bodies required special support timbering, and shafts burrowed fifteen hundred feet into the earth, journalist Dan DeQuille reported scores of ghastly accidents.

Falls accounted for the most horrifying deaths. Temperatures in the mines could reach 110 or 120 degrees; miners who shot to the surface in the lift after a long hot shift sometimes fainted and were torn to pieces when they fell out of the un-walled cages. About one such accident, DeQuille reported, "The trunk was rolled up in a piece of canvas and brought to the surface, while pieces of his arms, legs, and head were scraped up and sent up in candle-boxes." In his autobiography, DeQuille explained that, "It may be thought that I have selected the most shocking [accidents] I could find; but such is not the case." The statistics seem to bear him out. A careful cross-referencing of newspaper reports from 1863 to 1880 with mine rolls indicates that nearly one in ten miners was maimed or killed.

But mining was never the only opportunity at a gold strike. Within two months after the Camp brothers arrived in California with the Wolverine Rangers, they had stocked a store with sixteen thousand dollars worth of provisions, commenting for a hometown paper that, "We are sure to make money faster than we can dig it." Of the fifty-some men in their party, many worked only a few days in the diggings before setting upon a new career. As one Ranger commented, "Generally speaking the gold fever cools down in a wonderful manner after a man has been here a week or two."

Stories from the camps indicated that it was as easy to pluck gold from a person's palm as from the ground, and this was particularly attractive to women. Luzena Stanley Wilson, on her arrival in Nevada City, California, bought two planks and "with my own hands I chopped stakes, drove them into the ground, and set up my table. I bought provisions at a neighboring store, and when my husband

Casket in morgue, Bodie, California.
A partially constructed violin on the
table provides another example
of the woodworker's art.

came back at night he found, mid the weird light of the pine torches, twenty miners eating at my table." From then on, Mrs. Wilson served seventy-five to two hundred boarders at twenty-five dollars a week. She named her hotel El Dorado.

Other less conventional women sought opportunity on the mining frontier as well. The *Alta California* reported the landing of a shipload of what contemporary euphemism deemed the "fair but frail" in San Francisco harbor in May 1850. Working girls also arrived from Chile and Mexico, and were imported like chattel from China. Some, if their skins were the right color and they were particularly charming, earned a fabulous living. A night with a French woman in San Francisco in 1850 could cost four hundred dollars. Most women led more dismal lives. As journalist Sandra Dallas recorded:

"Most ended like Mabel Johnson [in Leadville, Colorado], a tired, aged dance hall performer who collapsed amid the catcalls and jibes of her drunken audience. She was carried to her shack in Tiger Alley where the whores and dance hall girls . . . brought in bread and cakes and set up a deathwatch. When it was over, [one of Mabel's women friends sighed], 'It was a blessed death.'"

✳ ✳ ✳

Blessed it might have seemed, for drug addiction and suicide ran rampant among prostitutes on the Western frontier.

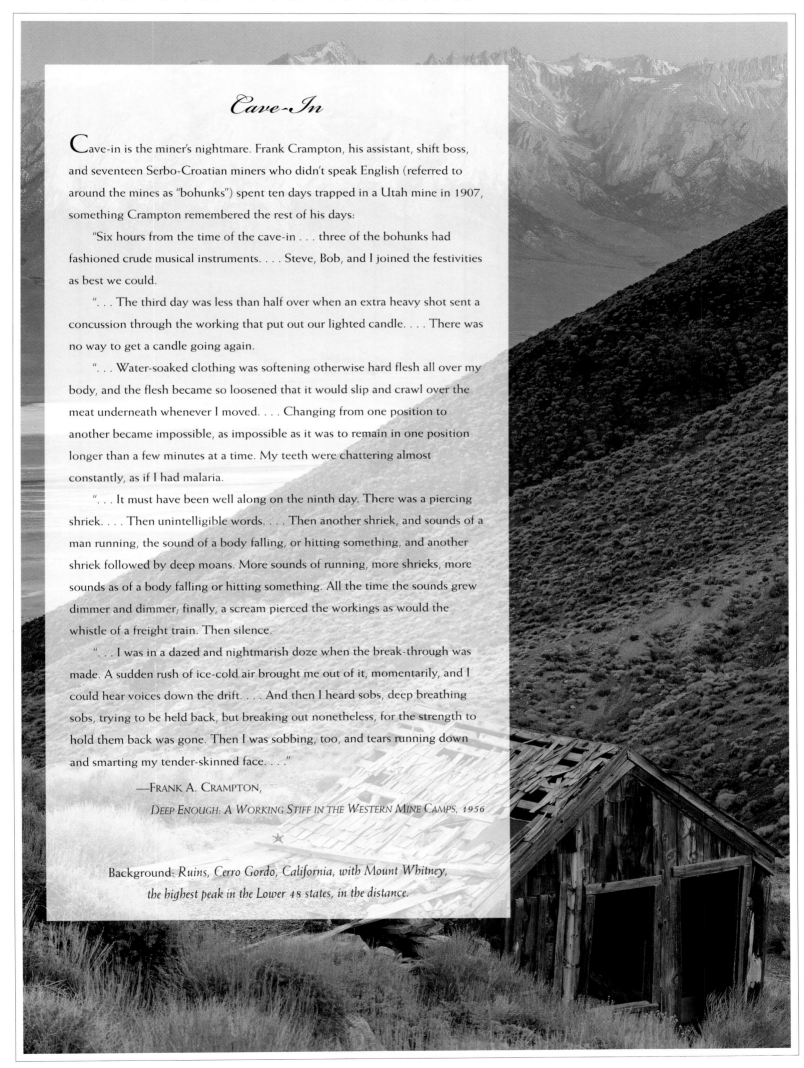

Cave-In

Cave-in is the miner's nightmare. Frank Crampton, his assistant, shift boss, and seventeen Serbo-Croatian miners who didn't speak English (referred to around the mines as "bohunks") spent ten days trapped in a Utah mine in 1907, something Crampton remembered the rest of his days:

"Six hours from the time of the cave-in . . . three of the bohunks had fashioned crude musical instruments. . . . Steve, Bob, and I joined the festivities as best we could.

". . . The third day was less than half over when an extra heavy shot sent a concussion through the working that put out our lighted candle. . . . There was no way to get a candle going again.

". . . Water-soaked clothing was softening otherwise hard flesh all over my body, and the flesh became so loosened that it would slip and crawl over the meat underneath whenever I moved. . . . Changing from one position to another became impossible, as impossible as it was to remain in one position longer than a few minutes at a time. My teeth were chattering almost constantly, as if I had malaria.

". . . It must have been well along on the ninth day. There was a piercing shriek. . . . Then unintelligible words. . . . Then another shriek, and sounds of a man running, the sound of a body falling, or hitting something, and another shriek followed by deep moans. More sounds of running, more shrieks, more sounds as of a body falling or hitting something. All the time the sounds grew dimmer and dimmer; finally, a scream pierced the workings as would the whistle of a freight train. Then silence.

". . . I was in a dazed and nightmarish doze when the break-through was made. A sudden rush of ice-cold air brought me out of it, momentarily, and I could hear voices down the drift. . . . And then I heard sobs, deep breathing sobs, trying to be held back, but breaking out nonetheless, for the strength to hold them back was gone. Then I was sobbing, too, and tears running down and smarting my tender-skinned face. . . ."

—FRANK A. CRAMPTON,
DEEP ENOUGH: A WORKING STIFF IN THE WESTERN MINE CAMPS, 1956

★

Background: *Ruins, Cerro Gordo, California, with Mount Whitney, the highest peak in the Lower 48 states, in the distance.*

*Above: General store,
Mogollon (pronounced "mogey-on"),
New Mexico. This structure received
a fresh coat of "weathered" paint when
it was used in a movie.
Right: Old gas pumps and truck,
Bodie, California.*

Whether one's talent ran to the licit or illicit, mining camps offered opportunity for anyone willing to work. Within a year of the first strike near Nome, Alaska, the camp-become-town boasted, according to historian Keith Wheeler, "twenty saloons, six bakeries, five laundries, twelve general merchandise stores, three secondhand stores, four wholesale liquor stores, three fruit, cigar and confectionery stores, two meat markets, one boat shop, a bookstore, a bank, two printing shops, four hotels, six restaurants, six lodging houses, four bathhouses, four barbershops,

Above: *The once-booming mining town of Placerville, Idaho, had a population of only fourteen by 1900; today its population is only about twice that, but it attracts many tourists in the summer.* Left: *Belmont, Nevada, was once the Nye County seat. Many structures remain today, including the courthouse in the distance.*

a hospital and a waterworks . . . and a demimonde that was growing so fast in number that no one bothered to count."

Every metal has magnetic properties; at least when discovered in rich enough quantities, it attracts miners, like bees to the hive, and they in turn attract a whirl of energy and industry. We frequently find old mining towns in high, windy places. Perhaps we only think they are windy. We just might be sensing the rush of industrious ghosts.

STRIKING IT RICH OR STRIKING OUT

✳

Left: *Collapsed building in Tomboy, Colorado.*
Above: *Torn curtains in Chloride, New Mexico.*

STRIKING IT RICH OR STRIKING OUT

Failure and Fortune in the Mining Camps

✳

I went to bed and dreamed of riches galore. . . .
My mind ran upon it all night long. I dreamed all sorts of things—
about a fine house and good clothes, a carriage and horses,
travel, what I would take to the folks down in old Missouri
and everything you can think of—I had struck it rich!
There were millions in it!"

—George Jackson, after he panned $10 worth of gold with

his tin cup from Clear Creek, Colorado, in 1859

"Land, cattle, horses,

everything began to

disappear. There is a saying

that men will steal

everything but a milestone

and a millstone. They

stole my millstones."

One of the ironies of the mining frontier is how many prominent figures in its history died penniless. James Marshall, who discovered gold in the American River and set off the California gold rush, "never earned a cent from his discovery." The fortunes of his once-prosperous employer, John Sutter, were even worse, for thousands of crazed gold seekers swarmed across his land, stealing everything in sight. As he later recalled, "Land, cattle, horses, everything began to disappear.

✳

Left: *Cemetery in Castleton, Utah, in the Castle Valley. Both the valley*
and the town take their name from Castle Rock, in the background.
Above: *The one-time resident of this shack in Belmont, Nevada, recycled his tin cans for siding.*

William Swain Goes Home

On November 4, 1850—almost a year to the day from his arrival in Sacramento Valley cold and hungry after the trials of Lassen's Cut-off—William Swain landed in San Francisco with $500 worth of gold dust in his pocket. It comprised all he had to show for the labor of his seventeen months away from New York, and he intended to use a good portion of it to buy a ticket home.

Swain had worked hard and forsworn drink and gambling, but like the vast majority of the California gold seekers, he had profited little. The frustration drove many insane. Swain, however, headed back to a welcoming family. "You have tried to do well," his brother reassured him. "To tell the plain truth, I wish most sincerely you were . . . at home, no matter if you haven't got a single mill."

Nor would Swain be sorry for his experience. "I have seen many hardships, dangers and privations, and made nothing by it . . ." he wrote from shipboard on the journey home, "but . . . I shall ever be glad that I have taken this trip. [What I have learned] will abundantly repay all my toils and privations, and . . . be a source of contentment and happiness both to myself and family and friends."

★

Background: *Jimsonweed, or sacred datura, Jerome, Arizona.*

✶

Above: *In 1880, the*
Tombstone Epitaph *published*
its first issue in which it made the point
that "no Tombstone is complete without
an Epitaph." Tombstone, site of the
famous "shoot-out at the O.K. Corral,"
is one of the most famous ghost towns
and also one of the most commercialized.
Left: *Casket in morgue, Bodie, California.*

There is a saying that men will steal everything but a milestone and a millstone.
They stole my millstones." Creditors took what the squatters and thieves left
behind; Sutter spent his final years broke and drunk, begging Congress to
compensate him "for having come to the aid of so many American emigrants and
for having once owned the land on which gold was found."

Nor did the four original owners of the Ophir Mine on Nevada's Comstock
Lode fare better. Irish immigrant Patrick McLaughlin sold out for $3,500 but died
penniless; his brother of the green, Peter O'Riley, garnered $45,000 but died in an
insane asylum. Old Virginny Finney supposedly traded his share for an "old horse,

✳

Above: *This church and cemetery in Golden, New Mexico, is in the Sandia Mountains on the old Turquoise Trail between Albuquerque and Santa Fe.*
Right: *Marietta, Nevada, is now part of a federally designated wild burro preserve; similar protection obviously does not extend to derelict cars.*
Far right: *Old rusted safe in Sandon, British Columbia.*

a pair of blankets, and a bottle of whiskey," drank up his profits, tumbled off his horse, and broke open his skull. The eponymous Henry T. P. Comstock, "Old Pancake," sold his share for $11,000 and promptly lost it. Always a blowhard, he remained colorful to the end, asserting that he still owned the mine and "with the grandiloquence of a King Lear announced that he was willing to allow his 'tenants' to live in Virginia City rent free, 'for the winters are cold and the people poor, and their need is greater than mine.'" He died by his own hand, and is buried in an unmarked grave in Bozeman, Montana.

Many individual prospectors did profit by their labors, especially those who

Overleaf: Tomboy, Colorado,
high above Telluride, was once one
of the richest gold mines in the district.
Above: In the last two decades of
the nineteenth century, Bay Horse,
Idaho, had rich silver reserves.
Today, it is closed to the public
because of vandalism.

knew when to quit. Stories like that of Moses and Fred Manuel are common. Twenty years after prospecting in California, they found a quartz vein south of Deadwood in the Black Hills which they named the Homestake and eventually sold with two other mines for $150,000. Like innumerable prospectors before them, they were happy enough. They were not greedy men, and they certainly couldn't underwrite the capital investment needed to fully exploit their finds. Their buyers could. San Francisco industrialists Lloyd Tevis, James Haggin, and George Hearst eventually put $650 million into mining operations in the Black Hills—and took more than one billion out.

But if few emigrant prospectors got rich themselves, the riches they discovered changed the West. California produced nearly $1.3 billion in gold by the turn of the century and its early wealth financed the Comstock Lode in Nevada, which in turn yielded $400 million and helped finance the Civil War and the building of the railroad. The six square miles of the Cripple Creek district in Colorado yielded $340 million in twenty-five years. The Klondike, with the help of industrial mining early in the twentieth century, offered up $300 million more. The map of the contemporary West has been carved in large part by picks and shovels and a lust for gold, which pushed settlement into the remotest regions and laced the continent with roads and rails.

What Dreams are Made Of

The men stepped into a wonderland of solid gold. The vug [cavity] was 20 feet long, 15 feet wide and 40 feet high. Its walls blazed with millions of gold crystals and 24-carat flakes as big as a thumbnail. Pure gold boulders littered the floor amid piles of white quartzlike spun glass. It was dreamlike wealth and beauty such as this that drove miners to delve into the earth."

—ROBERT WALLACE, *THE MINERS*, (IN DESCRIBING A FIND IN 1914 AT THE CRESSON MINE AT CRIPPLE CREEK, COLORADO, THAT YIELDED $1.2 MILLION IN A SINGLE MONTH)

Background: *Various minerals from Cerro Gordo, California.*

★

*Shaniko, Oregon, started out
life as a stage stop and developed
into an agricultural center for farmers
and ranchers. Today, tourists are
breathing new life into the town.*

Animals

Animals often figure into the lore surrounding mining camps. The Laramie, Wyoming, *Republican* reported in 1915 that one H. F. Williams had found gold in the crop of a bird he butchered for dinner. He killed five more, each of which yielded gold, and decided to hunt out the source of their grazing. "Inasmuch as the fowls have the run of a large field . . . by several dry ravines," reported the newspaper, "the search is not simple and has involved much labor which has been fruitless."

In the Coeur d'Alene district of northern Idaho, Noah Kellogg's jackass, on the other hand, proved a more provident prospector, at least according to legend. The critter made a habit of disappearing, and Kellogg had been searching for hours when he saw Old Jack stopped in his tracks on the side of a hill, his attention riveted on something across the canyon. Kellogg followed the ass's gaze and saw a "marvelous ore chute . . . reflecting the sun's rays like a mirror." The metal turned out to be galena, a mixture of lead and silver, in such quantity that the district eventually yielded $300 million. It's a grand story, even if undoubtedly false—galena tarnishes and would never have glinted "like a mirror."

More than one mining camp entrepreneur plotted ways to get rich through the labor of his four-legged friends. An outfit called the Trans-Alaskan Gopher Company set out to breed and train the rodents to tunnel in frozen tundra. Another Klondike entrepreneur carried crate after crate of cats over the backbreaking Chilkoot Pass in order to sell them for an ounce of gold apiece to miners tired of sharing their lodgings with mice. However whimsical such tales, the prospector's brutal life was often even harder on his animals. Klondike lore holds that horribly overloaded horses and mules on the White Pass Trail out of Skagway committed suicide by leaping from the cliffs to end their suffering, and photographs from the period record piles of overworked animals dead from exhaustion.

✳

Background: *Aspen leaves, Ironton, Colorado.*

✳

Situated in a narrow canyon in Utah's Oquirrh (pronounced "ochre") Mountains, Ophir has more vegetation than most Great Basin ghost towns.

Mining has left a complex legacy. The force of its passion displaced and devastated Native people, completely annihilating whole tribes. Hillsides hydraulicked away, and mountains denuded of trees carved scars in the land and damaged watersheds that haunt us today with such problems as endangered salmon runs in the Northwest and increasing desertification in Nevada.

"The rush to California . . . reflects the greatest disgrace on mankind," wrote Henry David Thoreau about that first great gold rush. "That so many are ready to live by luck and so get the means of commanding the labor of others less lucky, without contributing any value to society—and that's called enterprise!" But Thoreau's judgment was harsh. There were plenty who saw the Western lands simply as "a huge goose to be plucked at will," but many—probably the majority— simply wanted a chance to work hard for a better life.

"Oh, Matilda," wrote Captain David DeWolf in 1850, "oft is the night when laying alone on the hard ground with a blanket under me and one over me that my thoughts go back to Ohio and I think of you and wish myself with you. But I am willing to stand it all . . . so I can be independent of some of the darned sonabitches that felt themselves above me because I was poor." DeWolf and the thousands upon thousands like him hardly imagined the damage they were doing. What does a single raindrop know of the ravage of a flood?

Those who returned unrewarded rationalized their failure: at least, they had "seen the elephant." The phrase came from a popular story: A circus came to town and a farmer hurried to market; he had waited all his life to see an elephant and he finally had his chance. When he topped a hill, he met an elephant pulling a circus wagon. It terrified his horses and they bolted, spilling his produce and destroying his cart. "I don't give a hang!" the farmer said about his losses. "I have seen the elephant!"

Now, from the other side of the mining frontier, gazing back with the wisdom of hindsight, another, more contemporary elephant story—a children's riddle, really—might better tell the tale of that unstoppable force that peopled some one hundred thousand mining districts by 1900 and left so many of them empty a century later.

Where does an elephant sleep? Anywhere it wants to.

OTHER GHOSTS

★

Left: *Piedmont, Wyoming, once a railroad town.*
Above: *Crumbling barn door, Cloverdale, New Mexico.*

OTHER GHOSTS

Dreams, Droughts, and the Search for Home

As the Model T Ford took over from the horse and buggy,
and the town began to die, the livery barn came up for sale cheap. . . .
This was the first business to close but as time went on, people moved away
and others failed to take their places, the lumber yard burned down,
a tornado took the town hall, leaving the piano sitting forlornly in its place
with the sheet music still on the rack. Houses were moved away to other locations
and little by little the town just withered away like some plant that dries and
loses its leaves so slowly that the owner continues to hope for survival.

—PERCY WOLLASTON, *HOMESTEADING: A MONTANA FAMILY ALBUM,* 1997

✷

"A PILE OF GOLD-BEARING QUARTZ MARKED THE ROAD TO CALIFORNIA; THE OTHER ROAD HAD A SIGN BEARING THE WORDS 'TO OREGON.' THOSE WHO COULD READ TOOK THE TRAIL TO OREGON."

In the 1850s, a story circulated among Western emigrants. In the words of Dorothy O. Johansen, "At Pacific Springs, one of the crossroads of the Western trail, a pile of gold-bearing quartz marked the road to California; the other road had a sign bearing the words 'To Oregon.' Those who could read took the trail to Oregon."

✷

Left: *Old farm machinery, Capitol Reef National Park, Fruita, Utah.*
Above: *Old wagon, South Pass City, Wyoming.*

★

The one-time uranium mining town of Temple Mountain takes its name from the incredible peak behind it in Utah's San Raphael Swell.

✱

Paria, Utah, was built as a movie set two miles from the original Mormon town site of Pahreah in what is now the Grand Staircase–Escalante National Monument. Many episodes of Gunsmoke *as well as movies featuring actors from John Wayne to Sammy Davis Jr. were filmed here before a 1999 flood so damaged the set that it had to be torn down.*

In truth, the gold seekers were no less literate than their northering counterparts, but the story highlighted the divide between two fundamentally different types of people. Home and the land to build it on were all that mattered to the Oregon-bound travelers, and they expected to devote their lives to that end. Building a new home was the last thing on the gold seekers' minds; they wanted wealth and they wanted it quickly.

People migrate for a multitude of motives—for jobs, for wealth, for intellectual or religious freedom—but at least in the middle and late nineteenth and early twentieth centuries, more people headed West to find land of their own than for any other reason. The General Preemption Act of 1841 gave squatters claim to land without payment up front, and fifteen months to pay. The various Homestead Acts gave land outright to settlers if they lived on it for a designated period of time and made certain improvements. While many homesteaders relinquished their claims for quick profits and others pushed the rules to absurdity, nearly a million and a half homesteaders "proved out" between 1860 and 1920, accounting for a third of the new farms added to the census rolls during that period.

Homesteading, whether on a claim or paid for outright, was never easy—"In God we trusted; in Kansas we busted" ran one nineteenth-century ditty—and grew increasingly hard as settlers pushed past the 100th meridian. This line, which roughly bisected the Dakotas and Nebraska, and set off the Oklahoma panhandle and the western thirds of Kansas and Texas, demarked what author Mary Austin

later deemed the "Land of Little Rain." If common sense suggested that farming with less than fifteen inches of rain a year would prove hard if not impossible, the railroads and other developers promoted such pseudoscience as "rain follows the plow," and

A rock cabin and former camp site in Whitney Pockets, Nevada.

★

*Abandoned farm near Kent, Oregon.
Many one-time mining towns
have new leases on life because of their
mountain scenery; farm towns on
the prairie have a harder time.*

Iosepa, Utah

One of the more unusual Mormon ghost towns is Iosepa, twenty miles south of the Great Salt Lake, founded in 1889 by a group of Hawaiian converts who came to Salt Lake to be close to the Mormon Temple. Dry, windswept, and cold in winter, the sagebrush desert could hardly have been less hospitable to the islanders, but they developed an irrigation system, cultivated nearly twelve hundred acres, and planted hundreds of trees as well as grapes, raspberries, currants, and flowers, "amazing first-time visitors to the community who emerged from miles of barren desert into a virtual island oasis. . . ." The community became famous for its luaus and its musical groups, which performed around the state. But along with success at establishing a little of Hawaii's lushness came one of its scourges. In 1896, Hansen's disease—leprosy—broke out, and those affected were quarantined in a building a mile and a half from town, where all of them eventually died.

At its height, Iosepa's population numbered 228. It succeeded more as a spiritual challenge than as a comfortable home, and when the Mormon Church announced in 1916 that it was building a temple in Hawaii, almost all of the residents moved back home. But Iosepa comes alive again each Memorial Day, as Utah's Polynesian community gathers for a three-day festival near a memorial erected by the church and a towering statue of King Kamehameha, to place leis on the graves and celebrate the history of Iosepa.

★

Background: *Barn, Capitol Reef National Park, Utah.*

the Agassiz theory that locomotives create an electromagnetic attraction for rain. When these proved out as superstitions, they were replaced by Hardy Webster Campbell's gospel of dryland farming. It worked little better, a fact that prompted many bitter farmers to adopt the truism, "Dry farming works best in wet years."

Still, the promise of a Western home—increasingly accessible after the Central Pacific and Union Pacific Railroads met at Promontory Point, Utah, on May 10, 1869—lured millions, many coming out as individual families and others banding together in ethnic and national groups to found their own towns or agricultural colonies. African-Americans founded a dozen communities in Kansas in the years after the Civil War. Seven Jewish agricultural colonies developed in the state in the 1880s; the residents of Beersheba built their synagogue out of sod. The population of the Dakotas exploded during those years, rising from fourteen thousand non-Indian residents in 1870 to more than half a million in 1890, and whole towns sprang up that spoke only Swedish or Norwegian or German or Czech.

In Texas, towns established to serve the cattle drives "boomed and busted so quickly that censuses usually missed their peaks." Abilene, for instance, served the cattle trade for less than five years and only survived because of newly arriving

★

Fog in Whitney, Oregon. Whitney once served the eighty-mile narrow-gauge Sumpter Valley Railroad and supplied nearby mining towns with lumber cut in its seventy-five-employee sawmill.

farmers. Meanwhile, new settlements in Arizona, New Mexico, and southern Colorado had a distinctly Hispanic flavor as *Nuevomexicanos* spread out from the Rio Grande Valley, many of them trailing bands of sheep. Early settlers to Oregon saw

their numbers increase by the tens of thousands as the railroads brought trainloads
of hopeful homesteaders into the region.

The years between 1860 and 1920 saw unprecedented agricultural expansion.

Fort Laramie

Before towns dotted the American West, forts and trading posts sprang up, and Fort Laramie on the Laramie River in what is now Wyoming was typical. It started out life in 1834 as Fort William, the construction of fur trader William Sublette, and became a major fur-trading post after the American Fur Company purchased it two years later and eventually renamed it Fort Laramie.

By the time the fur trade petered out in the 1840s, the fort had become an important resupply point for settlers on the Oregon Trail, and its owners took quick advantage of the situation. A cup of sugar ran $1.50; a cup of flour $1.00. The historian Francis Parkman passed through in 1846 and noted, "I calculated the profits that accrued to the fort—and found that at the lowest estimate they exceeded eighteen hundred percent."

Fort Laramie had long served as a post office when in 1860 it became a major way station for the Pony Express. Nineteen months later it traded that franchise for a telegraph key when completion of the transcontinental line put the Pony Express out of business. The fort also served as a stop for the Deadwood Stage.

Fort Laramie experienced yet another incarnation as the Plains Indians rose against the flood of settlers and, in 1849, the U.S. government purchased the fort for a military outpost. It continued to serve in that capacity until 1890 when the Battle at Wounded Knee essentially ended Native American resistance. The Army decommissioned the fort and sold it at auction. Today the National Park Service administers it as a National Historic Site, and more than fifty thousand people a year visit the restored facility.

Background: *Bent's Old Fort National Historic Site,*
near the Arkansas River in Colorado.

New towns formed with each wave of eager settlers, and while agricultural
communities were more stable than those of the mining frontier, a drought,
depressed prices, or an irrigation scheme that fell through rang the death knell. The
Great Depression, which started ten years earlier for agriculture than for the rest of
the country, was particularly devastating, and the map of the West is littered with
the ghosts of hundreds of communities that died during the 1920s and 1930s.

    Percy Wollaston was five years old in 1909 when Congress passed the Enlarged
Homestead Act; the next year his parents took up a 320-acre homestead in remote,
eastern Montana near the new town of Mildred. The Milwaukee Road railway
promoted the rich soil and temperate climate with photographs of bountiful wheat
fields and voluptuous vegetables. The produce had actually been grown on irrigated
land near the Yellowstone River; the "temperate climate" turned out to include
drought and plagues of locusts. The Wollastons enjoyed a few good years—in
1912, Percy's father took an eighteen-pound turnip to Minnesota, which was
displayed in a bank window. But less than two decades later, the Wollastons—who
had held on longer than most—bowed to drought, debt, and forty-degree-below-
zero winters, and moved away.

    The railroads lured many west by hyperbole if not downright fraud, but other
communities formed out of sheer determination. Dearfield, Colorado, is a good

★

*Antelope Flats in Grand Teton
National Park, Wyoming, is a favorite
destination for bicyclists venturing out
from Jackson, twelve miles away.*

★

Left: *The railroad town of Piedmont,*
Wyoming, died after the construction of
a railway tunnel in 1901 changed the
route and trains no longer passed through.
Overleaf: Interior of barn, Fruita, Utah.
Page 109: Saddle room, Bodie,
California. These artifacts speak to a time
when horses powered the world.

example. Founded in 1910 by O. T. Jackson and his wife Minerva and based on the self-help philosophy of Booker T. Washington, the Negro Townsite and Land Company recruited homesteaders to settle about twenty-five miles east of Greeley. Dearfield was home to only seven families in 1911, and they nearly froze out. But by 1921, the *Weld County News* reported a thriving population of seven hundred, "with improved lands worth $750,000, livestock and poultry worth $200,000, and an annual production of $125,000." The Jacksons ran several businesses in town, including a gas station, a grocery store, a restaurant, and a dance hall. But drought and depression took their toll, and by 1942 the community was so deserted that Jackson offered it as a Japanese relocation camp. When that failed, Jackson tried to sell the town, again without success. When he died in 1948, he was the only resident, Minerva having died earlier.

For others, farmland in the West held out the promise not only of prosperity but also of spiritual grace. This was particularly true in Utah, settled by Mormons under the leadership of Brigham Young, who saw in the Great Basin an area so harsh and undesirable to others that his Latter Day Saints would be free of the persecution that had driven them from the East. Young prophesied that, through the efforts of his people, "the desert shall blossom as the rose," and Mormons founded some five hundred settlements in Utah and surrounding states between 1847 and 1900. By

★

Left: *Old threshing machine, Pinos Altos, New Mexico.* Above: *Weathered barn, Home of Truth, Utah. The religious cult that founded this community considered it the "navel of the universe."*

Metropolis, Nevada

It is said that all Hell needs is water and good company, and any number of development companies have promised as much about the desert through the years. In 1909, the Pacific Reclamation Company of New York set out to build a bit of heaven on forty thousand acres of sagebrush flatland in the northeast corner of Nevada. They called it Metropolis, and for a few short years it aspired to its name with a grand hotel, two parks, a brick schoolhouse, and an elaborate railroad depot with a fountain out front. Behind this transformation stood the promise of water in a towering dam, and nearly seven hundred residents came the first year. But the Pacific Reclamation Company had failed to secure water rights, which happened to reside with farmers downstream. The company went belly up in 1913, and most of the new residents left soon after, many losing everything they had.

In 1950, journalist Nell Murbarger visited Metropolis and asked one of its few residents, Mrs. William Glassman, why she had stayed. Glassman was nearly sixty, a "tiny wisp of a woman who wore faded blue jeans and a wide-brimmed hat." She remembered arriving on the train in Metropolis in 1913 at the age of twenty-two, and seeing handsome homesteads out the window and wind rippling through the grain fields like "waves running over a green ocean."

But then drought hit and "life became a nightmare of jackrabbits and range cattle, and litigation over water rights." Why did she stay? "I don't know," she answered. "Maybe we had to prove to ourselves that we were tougher than the ones who had left. Maybe we considered it sort of a challenge and wanted to show we could meet the desert on its own terms, and win! . . . I've asked myself . . . a thousand times . . . and I still don't know the answer!"

Nobody lives in Metropolis today, but the arched entryway to the school and the hotel's elevator shaft still stand, and you can locate the remains of a few foundations. Each Memorial Day, relatives—some of whom live in the area—come to the cemetery to decorate the graves.

★

Background: *Old house, Molson, Washington, near the Canadian border.*

sheer determination and will, many thrived under the most trying circumstances, but others burned out, washed away in flood, or turned to dust in drought.

The ghosts of farm towns carry a sadness that is largely missing in the mining towns. Mining was always a gamble—something that, in theory at least, paid out in adventure if not in success. The homesteaders wanted something more enduring. In 1994, Percy Wollaston's son Michel returned to the family homestead in Montana and located the foundation where the house had once stood. He also found a small medallion with a hinge attached. "I think I know what this is," he told a friend. "It's the clasp from an old-timey photograph album. They must have burned the family photos when they left." But while the leaving was so painful that the Wollastons wanted to blot out the fact that they had been there at all, Percy Wollaston later wrote about those years with tenderness and unromanticized affection.

The same forces that created ghost towns in the '20s and '30s had operated before, and they continue today. The farm towns wither when the crops fail or prices plummet or credit becomes too dear. The logging towns fall when the trees are cut down. The oil towns and gas towns and plutonium towns die when their riches are depleted. Overfishing kills the fishing and cannery villages. Each individual town, born of unique individuals, has a unique story, just as their histories all have something in common. The ghosts tell us where we've been, and speak their spectral warnings about the road ahead.

✳

A storm approaches an old wood grain elevator in Kent, Oregon.

EPILOGUE

★

Left: *Decaying wall in Elizabethtown, New Mexico.*
Above: *Adobe walls, Terlingua, Texas.*

EPILOGUE

Safeguarding the Ghosts

*You may see such . . . places, where only meadows and forests
are visible—and will find it hard to believe that there stood at one time
a fiercely-flourishing little city of one thousands souls . . . and
now nothing is left of it all but a lifeless, homeless solitude. . . .*

—MARK TWAIN, *ROUGHING IT*

GHOST TOWNS ARE
CRUCIBLES OF SORTS,
PLACES WHERE WE CAN
SEE THE REMNANTS OF
THE PAST AND ALSO FEEL
THEIR IMPLICATIONS IN
OUR VERY BONES.

History happened here," the great novelist Robert Penn Warren once said about his native South, by way of explaining the enduring appeal of the region's literature. I suspect ghost towns attract us for much the same reason. The history of the post-settlement American West is short—at less than two hundred years old, a mere footnote on the full span of human experience. Yet so much happened in so little time, and ghost towns are crucibles of sorts, places where we can see the remnants of the past and also feel their implications in our very bones.

Remnants open up to us like the pages of a book. When we find a rusty buttonhook bent under a rock, we hold in our hands the story of a weathered woman in calico whose life may well have been coming undone before her eyes.

Left: *Poppies bloom every year in Copperopolis, California.*
Above: *Fire station, Columbia, California.*

✳

Masonic Hall, Columbia,
California. Near the foothills
of the Sierra Nevada Range,
Columbia was the second-largest
city in California in the 1850s
and is now a California
State Historic Park.

★

*Decaying walls of the old
Town Hall, Elizabethtown, in the
Sangre de Cristo Mountains,
New Mexico. Elizabethtown was
the first town incorporated in
New Mexico Territory.*

When we stumble upon the ruins of a stamp mill, the travails of our own lives pale before the specter of miners and mules, struggling like slaves on the pyramids, hauling tons of iron up impossible passes to improbable places. The sound of a door creaking on a rusty hinge is a symphony of diligence, dreams, and desire syncopated by greed and grief.

When we read history in a book, we can be relatively sure that the text will be there when we next want it. If we lose our own copy, we can find another in a library. History written upon the land is more fragile, and its care rests in our own hands. We implore you: treat these ghosts like the living entities they are. Place that

Ruins at Rhyolite, Nevada.
Although enthusiastic boosters
built a railway station, the mines
played out before the railroad
reached the town.

buttonhook back beneath the rock; secure the swinging door from the wind. Take only photographs and consider, if you will, ways in which you might help to assure these ghost towns long life.

Almost all ghost towns rely on volunteers for their stabilization and renovation. If you have a favorite site, consider donating time or money to its local "friends" group. If no such group exists, you might consider starting one. And if you aren't able to actively aid in restoration, know that the ghosts appreciate your careful respect. They reach out to us from the past to the present. In turn we can lend a helping hand back across the years.

SOURCE NOTES

This work owes much to dozens of historians, researchers, and authors who have dedicated their lives to understanding the American West. Sources that have been of particular help by providing an overarching view of the West include *"It's Your Misfortune and None of My Own": A History of the American West* by Richard White (University of Oklahoma Press, 1991); *The Legacy of Conquest: The Unbroken Past of the American West* by Patricia Nelson Limerick (W. W. Norton, 1987); *The Oxford History of the American West* edited by Clyde A. Milner III, Carol A. O'Connor, and Martha A. Sandweiss (Oxford University Press, 1994); and *The Shaping of America, vol. 3, Transcontinental America, 1850–1915* by D. W. Meinig (Yale University Press, 1998). Two highly accessible popular works that have been valuable, by way of both their text and their excellent photographs, are *The West: An Illustrated History* by Geoffrey C. Ward (Little, Brown, 1996) and *The Miners* by Robert Wallace (Time-Life, 1976).

PROLOGUE (pp. 13–25)

The epigraph is from *Epigraph of Ghosts*, a stunning photo-essay on Midwestern farm towns with photographs by Bob Firth and text by Bill Holm (Voyageur Press, 1993).

GETTING THERE IS HALF THE FUN (pp. 27–39)

The epigraph as well as the information about William Swain came from *The World Rushed In: The California Gold Rush Experience* by J. S. Holliday (Simon & Schuster, 1981). This rich and fascinating book, arguably the most complete story of a single gold seeker, is drawn from Swain's journals and letters home and the letters his family wrote to him in return, and supplemented with diaries and letters from the other Wolverine Rangers who accompanied him. Ward tells Sam Brannan's story in *The West*. The details of the madness that overtook California and Oregon in the first days of the California gold rush are from *Ghost Towns and Mining Camps of California* by Remi Nadeau (Ward Richie Press, 1965). JoAnn Levy, in her excellent study *They Saw the Elephant: Women in the California Gold Rush* (Archon Books, 1990), provided the stories of the Bateses' coal ship adventures and the Briers' trip across Death Valley. Information on the trip across Panama came from T. H. Watkins's *Gold and Silver in the West* (Bonanza Books, 1971). Information about the devastating effects of gold rushes on Native populations came from Holliday, Ward, and Ken Burns and Robert Ives's 1996 PBS television series, *The West*.

HOME IS WHERE YOU HANG YOUR HAT (pp. 41–57)

Louisa Clapp, who wrote as Dame Shirley (*The Shirley Letters from the California Mines*, Alfred A. Knopf, 1965), was one of the most colorful chroniclers of the California gold rush. Both Holliday and Levy give examples of the poor health of miners, and Levy reprinted Dorothy Scraggs's personal ad. Nell Murbarger recorded J. Ross Browne's comments on Gila City in *Ghosts of the Adobe Walls* (Westernlore Press, 1964). Browne's description of Virginia City, Nevada, was quoted by Donald C. Miller in *Ghost Towns of Nevada* (Pruett Publishing Co., 1977). Sandra Dallas's *Colorado Ghost Towns and Mining Camps* (University of Oklahoma Press, 1985) offers a wealth of colorful detail, and the story about the winter-long poker game in Animas Forks, Colorado, as well as details about culture and

wealth, came from her book, as did the quotation from Anne Ellis. Ken and Ellen Sievert's *Virginia City and Alder Gulch* (Montana Magazine and American World Geographic Publishing, 1993) and Marilyn Grant's *A Guide to Historic Virginia City* (Montana Historical Society Press, 1998) are excellent resources. Watkins estimated the number of mining camps at one hundred thousand by 1900.

HI, HO! HI, HO! IT'S OFF TO WORK WE GO (pp. 59–73)

The epigraph from Swain came from *The World Rushed In* by Holliday. Both Wallace and Watkins are excellent sources for the technology of mining. Watkins cited the study correlating newspaper reports to injuries and deaths on the Comstock Lode. Levy tells the story of Luzena Stanley Wilson in Nevada City, California, and provides an excellent chapter on prostitutes in the California gold rush. Dan DeQuille's autobiography is riveting, full of colorful characters and horrifying details. Wheeler describes the flourishing of business in Nome, Alaska. Frank Crampton worked all over the mining West, and his autobiography, *Deep Enough: A Working Stiff in the Western Mine Camps* (University of Oklahoma Press, 1956/1982), is a jewel.

STRIKING IT RICH OR STRIKING OUT (pp. 75–89)

Wallace quotes George Jackson, provides information on the finders of the Ophir Mine on the Comstock Lode and the Manuel brothers in the Black Hills, and provides estimates of the yields of many gold mining regions. Ward tells the story of Sutter's later years and also quotes Captain David DeWolf. Almost everyone who writes about the mining frontier tells some version of "seeing the elephant." The one used here was based on Levy. Donald C. Miller mentioned the story of the gold-bearing geese in *Ghost Towns of Wyoming* (Pruett Publishing, 1977); Wallace told the stories of Old Jack in Idaho and the fate of animals in the Klondike.

OTHER GHOSTS (pp. 91–113)

Percy Wollaston's *Homesteading: A Montana Family Album* (Lyons Press, 1997) is an insightful and eloquent first-person narrative from the farming frontier. Allan G. Bogue's article "An Agricultural Empire," included in *The Oxford History of the American West* (edited by Milner et al., Oxford University Press, 1994), was invaluable to this chapter. Meinig quotes Dorothy O. Johansen. Stephen L. Carr's *The Historical Guide to Utah Ghost Towns* (Western Epics, 1972) is a good source for Mormon experience. Information on Iosepa came from "A History of Iosepa, Utah" by Richard Poulsen, published on the KUED public television website, www.kued.org/polynesian/history/index.html, and George A. Thompson's *Some Dreams Die: Utah's Ghost Towns and Lost Treasures* (Dream Garden Press, 1999). Nell Murbarger wrote about Metropolis, Nevada, in *Ghosts of the Glory Trail* (Nevada Publications, 1956). The University of Northern Colorado website, http://library.unco.edu/dearfld, provided information about Dearfield, Colorado.

EPILOGUE (pp. 115–123)

The epigraph is from *Roughing It* by Mark Twain (Harper & Brothers, 1959).

ADDITIONAL READING

GENERAL

Lambert Florin's *Ghost Towns of the West*, published in 1973 and reprinted in 1992 by Promontory Press, is dated now but, at nearly 900 pages and covering Alaska and the Yukon, Arizona, California, Colorado, Idaho, Montana, Nevada, New Mexico, Oregon, Texas, Utah, Washington, and Wyoming, it remains the single most comprehensive volume. It contains a wealth of stories and historical facts, but you will want to check other sources for updated maps and information on the conditions of towns you want to visit. Since URLs change all the time, simply type "ghost towns" into your search engine for dozens of websites.

The *Smithsonian Guide to Historic America* series, published by Stewart, Tabori & Chang, has volumes covering every region in the United States that are consistently rich with accurate historical information and beautiful photographs. They are organized to help the tourist set up comprehensive regional tours, and include information about museums and other historical sites as well as ghost towns. William Carter's *Sunset Ghost Towns of the West*, 2nd edition, published by Lane Publishing Company in 1978, has good information and wonderful photographs, as do all *Sunset Magazine* publications.

These sources will get you to ghost towns. To better understand what you are seeing once you get there, we highly recommend *The Mining Camps Speak: A New Way to Explore the Ghost Towns of the American West* by Beth and Bill Sagstetter (Benchmark Publishing of Colorado, 1998), which will help you learn to read the landscape, discovering the stories within even the sparsest remnants.

INDIVIDUAL STATES

There are literally hundreds of books focused on individual states, counties, and towns. Local bookstores are rich sources and can often lead you to publications specific to your interest. In addition to those already listed among the general sources, here are a few we think are especially helpful.

ALASKA

Ron Wendt, *Gold, Ghost Towns and Grizzlies: Treasure Hunting in Alaska*, Goldstream Publications, 1995.

George Herben, *Picture Journeys in Alaska's Wrangell–St. Elias, America's Largest Park*, Alaska Northwest Books, 1997 (information on the town of Kennicott).

ARIZONA

Philip Varney, *Arizona's Ghost Towns and Mining Camps: A Travel Guide to History*, Arizona Highways, 1998.

CALIFORNIA

Bodie State Historic Park [visitor brochure], California State Parks, 1988, rev. 1999.

Mary Dedecker et al., *Death Valley to Yosemite: Frontier Mining Camps & Ghost Towns: The Men, The Women, Their Mines and Stories*, Spotted Dog Press, 1998.

Philip Varney, *Southern California's Best Ghost Towns: A Practical Guide*, University of Oklahoma Press, 1990.

Remi A. Nadeau, *Ghost Towns and Mining Camps of California: A History and Guide*, Crest Publishers, 1999.

COLORADO

Perry Eberhart, *Ghosts of the Colorado Plains*, Ohio University Press, 1996.

Philip Varney, *Ghosts Towns of Colorado: Your Guide to Colorado's Historic Mining Camps and Ghost Towns*, Voyageur Press, 1999.

THE DAKOTAS

Watson Parker, *Black Hills Ghost Towns*, Swallow Press, 1986.

Donald C. Miller, *Ghosts of the Black Hills*, Pictorial Histories Publishing Company, 1996.

IDAHO

Wayne Sparling, *Southern Idaho Ghost Towns*, Caxton Printers, 1981.

MONTANA

Don C. Miller, *Ghost Towns of Montana*, Pruett Publishing, 1991.

Muriel Sibell Wolle, *Montana Pay Dirt: A Guide to the Mining Camps of the Treasure State*, Ohio University Press, 1991.

NEVADA

Shawn Hall, several comprehensive books on individual counties, University of Nevada Press, 1990s.

NEW MEXICO

Philip Varney, *New Mexico's Best Ghost Towns: A Practical Guide*, University of New Mexico Press, 1987.

OREGON AND WASHINGTON

Norman D. Weis, *Ghost Towns of the Northwest*, Caxton Printers, 1993.

Kenneth A. Erickson, *Lumber Ghosts: A Travel Guide to the Historic Lumber Towns of the Pacific Northwest*, Pruett Publishing, 1994.

Ruth Kirk and Carmela Alexander, *Exploring Washington's Past: A Road Guide to History*, University of Washington Press, 1995.

TEXAS

T. Lindsay Baker, *Ghost Towns of Texas*, University of Oklahoma Press, 1991.

UTAH

George A. Thompson, *Some Dreams Die: Utah's Ghost Towns and Lost Treasures*, Dream Garden Press, 1999.

INDEX